The Last Will and Testament of

JACQUELINE KENNEDY ONASSIS

The Last Will and Testament of

JACQUELINE KENNEDY ONASSIS

A BILL ADLER BOOK

Carroll & Graf Publishers, Inc.
New York

First Carroll & Graf edition 1997

Carroll & Graf Publishers, Inc.
260 Fifth Avenue
New York, NY 10001

Onassis, Jacqueline Kennedy, 1929-1994
    The last will and testament of Jacqueline Kennedy Onassis. — 1st Carroll & Graf ed.
        p. cm.
    "A Bill Adler book."
    ISBN 0-7867-0402-0
    1. Onassis, Jacqueline Kennedy, 1929-1994 — Will.   2. Onassis, Jacqueline Kennedy, 1929-1994 — Estate.   I. Title.
CT275.0552L37 1997
973.922'092—dc21
    [B]   97-3484
                                                                                    CIP

Manufactured in the United States of America

The Last Will and Testament of

JACQUELINE KENNEDY ONASSIS

Who's Who in the Will

Rachel (Bunny) L. Mellon	*longtime friend of Jacqueline Kennedy Onassis, who designed the Rose Garden at the White House*
Maurice Tempelsman	*companion*
Alexander D. Forger	*attorney and friend*
Caroline B. Kennedy	*daughter*
John F. Kennedy, Jr.	*son*
Lee B. Radziwill	*sister*
Nancy T. Tuckerman	*longtime friend and confidante*
Marta Squbin	*governess for Caroline Kennedy and John F. Kennedy, Jr.*
Alexandra Rutherfurd	*niece*
Providencia Pardes	*Jacqueline Kennedy Onassis's personal maid while she was in the White House*
Lee Nasso	*accountant*
Marie Amaral	*personal maid*
Efigenio Pinheiro	*butler at Fifth Avenue apartment*
Hugh D. Auchincloss, Jr.	*stepbrother*
Michel Bouvier	*cousin*
Anna Christina Radziwill	*daughter of Lee B. Radziwill, Jacqueline Kennedy Onassis's sister*
Anthony Radziwill	*son of Lee B. Radziwill*

Editor's Note: Following is a facsimile
of the original will. All handwritten
markings are on the actual document.
No editorial changes have been made.

THE WILL

(Probate Decree)

At Chambers of the Surrogate's Court of the State
of New York, held in and for the, County of New
York, at the Courthouse, New York on

JUNE , 19 **94**

PRESENT:

HON. **EVE PREMINGER,**
Surrogate

<table>
<tr><td>

Probate proceeding, Will of

JACQUELINE K. ONASSIS,

Deceased.

</td><td>

DECREE GRANTING PROBATE

File No. 2219-94

</td></tr>
</table>

SATISFACTORY PROOF having been made that jurisdiction has been obtained of all necessary parties and that all necessary notice has been given; AND the witnesses to said last Will bearing date March 22, 1994 having been sworn and examined, their examination having been reduced to writing and filed, or their affidavits having been filed, and it appearing by such proof that said Will was duly executed, and that the Testatrix at the time of executing it was in all respects competent to make a Will, and not under restraint, and the Court being satisfied of the genuineness of the said will of Jacqueline K. Onassis and the validity of its execution:

IT IS ORDERED, ADJUDGED AND DECREED, that the instrument offered for probate herein be, and the same hereby is, admitted to probate as the Will of said Jacqueline K. Onassis , deceased, valid to pass real and personal property, and that the said Will and this decree be recorded, and that letters testamentary be issued to the executors and letters of Trusteeship and trustees , who may qualify thereunder.

Eve Preminger
Surrogate

I, JACQUELINE K. ONASSIS, of the City, County and State of New York, do make, publish and declare this to be my Last Will and Testament, hereby revoking all wills and codicils at any time heretofore made by me.

FIRST: A. I give and bequeath to my friend RACHEL (BUNNY) L. MELLON, if she survives me, in appreciation of her designing the Rose Garden in the White House my Indian miniature "Lovers watching rain clouds," Kangra, about 1780, if owned by me at the time of my death, and my large Indian miniature with giltwood frame "Gardens of the Palace of the Rajh," a panoramic view of a pink walled garden blooming with orange flowers, with the Rajh being entertained in a pavilion by musicians and dancers, if owned by me at the time of my death.

B. I give and bequeath to my friend MAURICE TEMPELSMAN, if he survives me, my Greek alabaster head of a woman if owned by me at the time of my death.

ATTY.

C. I give and bequeath to my friend ALEXANDER D. FORGER, if he survives me, my copy of John F. Kennedy's Inaugural Address signed by Robert Frost if owned by me at the time of my death.

D. Except as hereinabove otherwise effectively bequeathed I give and bequeath all my tangible personal property, including, without limitation, my collection of letters, papers and documents, my personal effects, my furniture, furnishings, rugs, pictures, books, silver, plate, linen, china, glassware, objects of art, wearing apparel, jewelry, automobiles and their accessories, and all other household goods owned by me at the time of my death to my children who survive me, to be divided between them by my Executors, in the exercise of sole and absolute discretion, in as nearly equal portions as may be practicable, having due regard for the personal preferences of my children.

I authorize and empower my children, within a period of nine (9) months from the date of my death, to renounce and disclaim all interest in any part or all of the tangible personal property bequeathed to them pursuant to this Paragraph D of Article FIRST. Any such disclaimer shall be by instrument in writing, duly executed and filed in the court in which this Will has been admitted to original probate.

E. Any interests in my tangible personal property which are disclaimed by my children shall be disposed of as follows:

1. I give and bequeath such items of said tangible personal property and interests therein which relate to the life and work of my late husband, John F. Kennedy, to JOHN FITZGERALD KENNEDY LIBRARY INCORPORATED, Boston, Massachusetts, or if said library shall not be a qualified charitable beneficiary, as defined in Paragraph A of Article SECOND hereof, at the time of my death, to such one or more qualified charitable beneficiaries with similar purposes as my Executors, in the exercise of sole and absolute discretion, shall select.

2. I direct that the balance of said tangible personal property shall be sold and the net proceeds of sale shall be added to my residuary estate, thereafter to be held, administered and disposed of as a part thereof.

F. I give and bequeath all copyright interests owned by me at the time of my death in my personal papers, letters or other writings by me, including any royalty or other rights with respect thereto, to my children who survive me, in equal shares. I request, but do not direct, my children to respect my wish for privacy with respect to such papers, letters and writings and, consistent with that wish, to take whatever action is warranted to prevent the display, publication or distribution, in whole or in part, of these papers, letters and writings.

2

SECOND: A. I have made no provision in this my Will for my sister, Lee B. Radziwill, for whom I have great affection because I have already done so during my lifetime. I do wish, however, to remember her children and, thus, I direct my Executors to set aside the amount of Five Hundred Thousand Dollars ($500,000) for each child surviving me of my sister, Lee B. Radziwill, and I give and bequeath the sum so set aside to the Trustees hereinafter named, IN TRUST, NEVERTHELESS, to hold the same, and to manage, invest and reinvest the same, to collect the income thereof and to dispose of the net income and principal for the following uses and purposes and subject to the following terms and conditions:

1. Payment of Annuity Amount. The Trustees shall hold and manage the trust property for a term (the "trust term") which shall commence with the date of my death and shall end on the tenth (10th) anniversary thereof. At the end of each taxable year of the trust during the trust term (other than any short taxable year thereof for which specific provisions are hereinafter made), the Trustees shall pay over to such organization or organizations, to be selected by the Trustees, in the exercise of sole and absolute discretion, and only to such organization or organizations as are described in and satisfy the requirements of both of sections 170(c) and 2055(a) of the Internal Revenue Code of 1986, as amended (hereinafter sometimes referred to as the "Code"), at the time any such payment or payments to such organization or organizations are made (such organization or organizations shall herein be referred to collectively as the "qualified charitable beneficiaries") in such amounts or proportions, equal or unequal, as the Trustees, in the exercise of sole and absolute discretion, shall determine, such amount or amounts as shall, in the aggregate, equal ten percent (10%) of the initial net fair market value of the trust assets as finally

3

determined for federal estate tax purposes. Such aggregate amount shall hereinafter be referred to as the "annuity amount."

The annuity amount shall be paid first from the ordinary taxable income of the trust (including short term capital gains) which is not unrelated business income and, to the extent not so satisfied, the annuity amount shall be paid from the long term capital gains, the unrelated business income, the tax exempt income and finally out of the principal of the trust, in that order. In any taxable year of the trust in which the net income exceeds the annuity amount, the excess, at the end of such taxable year, shall be added to trust principal and thereafter shall be held, administered and disposed of as a part thereof. Should the initial net fair market value of the assets comprising the trust, and hence the annuity amount, be incorrectly determined, then within a reasonable period after the value of such assets is finally determined for federal tax purposes, the Trustees shall pay over to the qualified charitable beneficiaries, in the case of an undervaluation, or, in the case of an overvaluation, shall receive from such beneficiaries to which amounts from the trust were paid, in proportion to the payments made to each, an aggregate amount equal to the difference between the annuity amount properly payable and the annuity amount actually paid during such taxable year.

2.   <u>Distribution at End of Trust Term</u>.   Upon the expiration of the trust term, the trust created under this Paragraph A shall terminate, and the Trustees shall thereupon transfer, convey and pay over the trust assets, as they are then constituted (other than any amount due to the qualified charitable beneficiaries), to the then living descendants of my sister, Lee B. Radziwill, <u>per stirpes</u>.

3.   <u>Proration of Annuity Amount</u>.   To determine the proper aggregate amount payable from the trust to the qualified

4

charitable beneficiaries in any short taxable year of the trust's existence, the Trustees shall prorate the annuity amount, on a daily basis, in accordance with the applicable provisions of Treas. Dept. Reg. § 1.664-2.

4. _Deferral Provision_. The obligation to pay the annuity amount to the qualified charitable beneficiaries shall commence with the date of my death, but payment of the annuity amount may be deferred from the date of my death until the end of the taxable year of the trust in which occurs the complete funding of the trust. Within a reasonable time after the end of the taxable year in which complete funding of the trust occurs, the Trustees shall pay to the qualified charitable beneficiaries, in the case of an underpayment, or shall receive from the qualified charitable beneficiaries, in the case of an overpayment, in proportion to the payments made to each, the difference between: (1) any annuity amounts actually paid, plus interest, compounded annually, computed for any period at the rate of interest that the Treasury Regulations under section 664 of the Code prescribe for the trust for such computation for such period, and (2) the annuity amounts properly payable, plus interest, compounded annually, computed for any period at the rate of interest that the Treasury Regulations under section 664 of the Code prescribe for the trust for such computation for such period.

5. _Additional Contributions_. No additional contribution shall be made to the trust after the initial contribution which shall consist of all property passing to the trust by reason of my death.

6. _Prohibited Transactions_. Notwithstanding any other provision in this my Will, during the trust term, the Trustees are expressly prohibited (a) from engaging in any act of self-dealing as defined in section 4941(d) of the Code, (b) from retaining any

5

excess business holdings as defined in section 4943(c) of the Code which would subject the trust to tax under section 4943 of the Code, (c) from making any investments which would subject the trust to tax under section 4944 of the Code, and (d) from making any taxable expenditures as defined in section 4945(d) of the Code. The Trustees shall make distributions at such time and in such manner as not to subject the trust to tax under section 4942 of said Code.

7. <u>Taxable Year; Code References</u>. As used in this Paragraph A, the term "taxable year" of the trust shall mean the calendar year and the term "initial net fair market value" of the trust assets shall mean the initial net fair market value of those assets as the term is used in section 664(d)(1) of the Code. All references to sections of the Code and the regulations and rulings issued thereunder in this Paragraph A shall be deemed to include future amendments to such sections, regulations and rulings as well as corresponding provisions of future Internal Revenue laws, regulations and rulings.

8. <u>Intention</u>. It is my intention to insure that the interest committed to the qualified charitable beneficiaries by this Paragraph A shall be deductible for income and estate tax purposes under the provisions of the Code. Further, I intend that payments of gross income made by the Trustees to qualified charitable beneficiaries qualify as income tax charitable deductions. Accordingly, I direct that all provisions of this Paragraph A and this my Will shall be construed to effectuate this intention, that all provisions of this Paragraph A and this my Will shall be construed, and the trust be administered, solely in a manner consistent with sections 170(c), 642(c), and 2055 of the Code, and with regulations and rulings which may be promulgated from time to time with respect to trusts creating charitable interests, that none of the powers granted to the Trustees by this my Will shall be

6

exercised in a manner as to disqualify the trust for such deductions, and specifically, but without limiting the foregoing, that nothing in this my Will shall be construed to restrict the Trustees from investing the trust assets in a manner which could result in the annual realization of a reasonable amount of income or gain from the sale or disposition of trust assets. I hereby grant to my Executors and the Trustees all the administrative powers necessary to act in compliance with the requirements of the Code, as in effect at the time of my death and from time to time thereafter, so as to qualify the interest committed to the qualified charitable beneficiaries hereunder for the estate and income tax charitable deductions. Should any provisions of this my Will be inconsistent or in conflict with the sections of the Code and the regulations and rulings governing charitable lead trusts as in effect from time to time, then such sections, regulations and rulings shall be deemed to override and supersede such inconsistent or conflicting provisions. If such sections, regulations and rulings at any time require that instruments creating charitable lead trusts contain provisions which are not expressly set forth in this my Will, then such provisions shall be incorporated herein by reference and shall be deemed to be a part of this my Will to the same extent as though they had been expressly set forth herein.

9. <u>Trustees' Limited Power of Amendment</u>. The Trustees shall have the power, acting alone, to amend the provisions governing this trust contained in this my Will in any manner required for the sole purpose of ensuring that the trust qualifies and continues to qualify as a charitable lead annuity trust.

B. I give and bequeath the amount of Two Hundred and Fifty Thousand Dollars ($250,000) to each child of mine who survives me.

C. I give and bequeath to NANCY L. TUCKERMAN, if she survives me, the amount of Two Hundred and Fifty Thousand Dollars ($250,000).

D. I give and bequeath to MARTA SGUBIN, if she survives me, the amount of One Hundred and Twenty-Five Thousand Dollars ($125,000).

E. I give and bequeath to my niece ALEXANDRA RUTHERFURD, if she survives me, the amount of One Hundred Thousand Dollars ($100,000).

F. I give and bequeath to PROVIDENCIA PAREDES, if she survives me, the amount of Fifty Thousand Dollars ($50,000).

G. I give and bequeath to LEE NASSO, if she survives me, the amount of Twenty-Five Thousand Dollars ($25,000).

H. I give and bequeath to MARIE AMARAL, if she survives me, the amount of Twenty-Five Thousand Dollars ($25,000).

I. I give and bequeath to EFIGENIO PINHEIRO, if he survives me, the amount of Twenty-Five Thousand Dollars ($25,000).

THIRD: A. I give and devise any and all interest owned by me at the time of my death in the real property located in the City of Newport, State of Rhode Island, which I inherited from my mother, Janet Lee Auchincloss, and which is known as "Hammersmith Farm," including all buildings thereon and all rights and easements appurtenant thereto and all policies of insurance relating thereto, to HUGH D. AUCHINCLOSS, JR., if he survives me, or, if he does not survive me, to his children who survive me, in equal shares as tenants-in-common.

B. I give and devise all real property owned by me at the time of my death and located in the Towns of Gay Head and Chilmark, Martha's Vineyard, Massachusetts, including all buildings thereon and all rights and easements appurtenant thereto and all policies of

8

insurance relating thereto, to my children who survive me, in equal shares as tenants-in-common, or, if only one of my children survive me, to such survivor, or, if none of my children survive me, I authorize, but do not direct, my Executors to sell such real property and I direct that the net proceeds of sale together with any such real property not so sold be added to my residuary estate to be held, administered and disposed of as a part thereof.

I authorize and empower my children, within a period of nine (9) months from the date of my death, to renounce and disclaim all interest in any part or all of said real property devised to them pursuant to this Paragraph B of Article THIRD. Any such disclaimer shall be by instrument in writing, duly executed and filed in the court in which this Will has been admitted to original probate.

I direct that any such interest in my real property in Martha's Vineyard, Massachusetts which is disclaimed by my children shall be sold, and the net proceeds of sale shall be added to my residuary estate, thereafter to be held, administered and disposed of as a part thereof.

C. Except as hereinbefore otherwise effectively devised, I give and devise all real property owned by me at the time of my death, including all buildings thereon and all rights and easements appurtenant thereto and all policies of insurance relating thereto, to my children who survive me, in equal shares as tenants-in-common, or, if only one of my children survive me, to such survivor, or, if none of my children survive me, I authorize, but do not direct, my Executors to sell any such real property and I direct that the net proceeds of sale together with any such property not so sold be added to my residuary estate and thereafter held, administered and disposed of as a part thereof.

I authorize and empower my children, within a period of nine (9) months from the date of my death, to renounce and disclaim

9

all interest in any part or all of said real property devised to them pursuant to this Paragraph C of Article THIRD. Any such disclaimer shall be by instrument in writing, duly executed and filed in the court in which this Will has been admitted to original probate.

I direct that any such interest in my real property which is disclaimed by my children shall be sold, and the net proceeds of sale shall be added to my residuary estate, thereafter to be held, administered and disposed of as a part thereof.

D. I give, devise and bequeath all stock owned by me at the time of my death in any corporation which is the owner of any building in which I have a cooperative apartment, together with any lease to such apartment and all right, title and interest owned by me at the time of my death in and to any agreements relating to said building and the real property on which it is located, to my children who survive me, in equal shares as tenants in common, or, if only one of my children survive me, to such survivor, or, if none of my children survive me, I authorize, but do not direct, my Executors to sell any such stock and I direct that the net proceeds of sale together with any such stock not so sold be added to my residuary estate and thereafter held, administered and disposed of as a part thereof.

I authorize and empower my children, within a period of nine (9) months from the date of my death, to renounce and disclaim all interest in any part or all of said stock devised to them pursuant to this Paragraph D of Article THIRD. Any such disclaimer shall be by instrument in writing, duly executed and filed in the court in which this Will has been admitted to original probate.

I direct that any such interest in said stock which is disclaimed by my children shall be sold, and the net proceeds of sale shall be added to my residuary estate, thereafter to be held, administered and disposed of as a part thereof.

10

CHILDREN ARE TAKEN IN DEFAULT OF EXERCISE. BOTH WAIVE

FOURTH: Under the Will of my late husband, John Fitzgerald Kennedy, a marital deduction trust was created for my benefit over which I was accorded a general power of appointment. I hereby exercise such power of appointment and direct that, upon my death, all property subject to such power be transferred, conveyed and paid over to my descendants who survive me, per stirpes.

FIFTH: All the rest, residue and remainder of my property and estate, both real and personal, of whatsoever kind and wheresoever situated, of which I shall die seized or possessed or of which I shall be entitled to dispose at the time of my death (my "residuary estate"), after the payment therefrom of the taxes directed in Article NINTH hereof to be paid from my residuary estate (my "net residuary estate"), I give, devise and bequeath to the Trustees hereinafter named, IN TRUST, NEVERTHELESS, to hold as THE C & J FOUNDATION (sometimes hereinafter referred to as the "Foundation") and to manage, invest and reinvest the same, to collect the income thereof and to dispose of the net income and principal thereof for the following uses and purposes subject to the following terms and conditions:

A. 1. Payment of Annuity Amount. The Trustees shall hold and manage the Foundation property for a primary term which shall commence with the date of my death and shall end on the 24th anniversary thereof. [In no event, however, shall the Foundation's primary term extend beyond a period of twenty-one (21) years after the death of the last to die of those descendants of my former father-in-law Joseph P. Kennedy who were in being at the time of my death.] At the end of each taxable year of the Foundation during the primary term (other than any short taxable year thereof for which specific provisions are hereinafter made), the independent Trustees (i.e., the Trustees of the Foundation other than any Trustee who has

11

disclaimed any property of my Estate which becomes a part of the Foundation) shall pay over to such organization or organizations, to be selected by the independent Trustees, in the exercise of sole and absolute discretion, and only to such organization or organizations as are described in and satisfy the requirements of both of sections 170(c) and 2055(a) of the Code, at the time any such payment or payments to such organization or organizations are made (such organization or organizations shall herein be referred to collectively as the "qualified charitable beneficiaries") in such amounts or proportions, equal or unequal, as the independent Trustees, in the exercise of sole and absolute discretion, shall determine, such amount or amounts as shall, in the aggregate, equal eight percent (8%) of the initial net fair market value of the assets of the Foundation as finally determined for federal estate tax purposes. Such aggregate amount shall hereinafter be referred to as the "annuity amount."

The annuity amount shall be paid first from the ordinary taxable income of the Foundation (including short term capital gains) which is not unrelated business income and, to the extent not so satisfied, the annuity amount shall be paid from the long term capital gains, the unrelated business income, the tax exempt income and finally out of the principal of the trust, in that order. In any taxable year of the Foundation in which the net income exceeds the annuity amount, the excess, at the end of such taxable year, shall be added to the principal of the Foundation and thereafter shall be held, administered and disposed of as a part thereof. Should the initial net fair market value of the assets comprising the Foundation, and hence the annuity amount, be incorrectly determined, then within a reasonable period after the value of such assets is finally determined for federal tax purposes, the Trustees shall pay over to the qualified charitable beneficiaries, in the case of an

12

undervaluation, or, in the case of an overvaluation, shall receive from such beneficiaries to which amounts from the Foundation were paid, in proportion to the payments made to each, an aggregate amount equal to the difference between the annuity amount properly payable and the annuity amount actually paid during such taxable year.

I have accorded the independent Trustees sole and absolute discretion in selecting the qualified charitable beneficiaries to receive all or any portion of the annuity amount referred to in this Paragraph A of Article FIFTH, stipulating only that at the time any payment from the Foundation is made to a qualified charitable beneficiary so selected it be an organization described in sections 170(c) and 2055(a) of the Code. It is my wish, however, that in selecting the particular qualified charitable beneficiaries which shall be the recipients of benefits from the Foundation the independent Trustees give preferential consideration to such eligible organization or organizations the purposes and endeavors of which the independent Trustees feel are committed to making a significant difference in the cultural or social betterment of mankind or the relief of human suffering. To assist the independent Trustees I authorize, but do not direct, that they retain my close friend and confidante Nancy L. Tuckerman to assist them in the administration of the Foundation. Should the independent Trustees deem it advisable to retain Nancy L. Tuckerman, they shall pay to her from the assets of the Foundation reasonable compensation for the services she shall render. But such compensation shall not be charged against the annuity amount in any full taxable year of the Foundation nor against the appropriate fraction of said amount, determined as herein provided, payable to the qualified charitable beneficiaries in any short taxable year of the Foundation but shall rather be paid from the assets of the Foundation at large.

13

2.   Proration of the Annuity Amount.   To determine
the proper aggregate amount payable from the Foundation to the
qualified charitable beneficiaries in any short taxable year of the
Foundation's existence, the independent Trustees shall prorate the
annuity amount, on a daily basis, in accordance with the applicable
provisions of Treas. Dept. Reg. § 1.664-2.

3.   Deferral Provision.   The obligation to pay the
annuity amount to the qualified charitable beneficiaries shall
commence with the date of my death, but payment of the annuity amount
may be deferred from the date of my death until the end of the
taxable year of the Foundation in which occurs the complete funding
of the Foundation.   Within a reasonable time after the end of the
taxable year in which complete funding of the Foundation occurs, the
independent Trustees shall pay to the qualified charitable
beneficiaries, in the case of an underpayment, or shall receive from
the qualified charitable beneficiaries, in the case of an
overpayment, in proportion to the payments made to each, the
difference between (1) any annuity amounts actually paid, plus
interest, compounded annually, computed for any period at the rate of
interest that the Treasury Regulations under section 664 of the Code
prescribe for the Foundation for such computation during such period,
and (2) the annuity amounts properly payable, plus interest,
compounded annually, computed for any period at the rate of interest
that the Treasury Regulations under section 664 of the Code prescribe
for the Foundation for such computation during such period.

4.   Additional Contributions.   No additional
contributions shall be made to the Foundation after the initial
contribution which shall consist of all property passing to the
Foundation by reason of my death.

5.   Prohibited Transactions.   Notwithstanding any
other provision in this my Will, during the primary term, the

Trustees are expressly prohibited (a) from engaging in any act of self-dealing as defined in section 4941(d) of the Code, (b) from retaining any excess business holdings as defined in section 4943(c) of the Code which would subject the Foundation to tax under section 4943 of the Code, (c) from making any investments which would subject the Foundation to tax under section 4944 of the Code, and (d) from making any taxable expenditures as defined in section 4945(d) of the Code. The Trustees shall make distributions at such time and in such manner as not to subject the Foundation to tax under section 4942 of the Code.

6. <u>Taxable Year; Code References</u>. As used in this Paragraph A, the term "taxable year" of the Foundation shall mean the calendar year and the term "initial net fair market value" of the assets of the Foundation shall mean the initial net fair market value of those assets as the term is used in section 664(d)(1) of the Code. All references to sections of the Code and the regulations and rulings issued thereunder in this Paragraph A shall be deemed to include future amendments to such sections, regulations and rulings as well as corresponding provisions of future Internal Revenue laws, regulations and rulings.

7. <u>Intention</u>. It is my intention to insure that the interest committed to the qualified charitable beneficiaries by this Paragraph A shall be deductible for income and estate tax purposes under the provisions of the Code. Further, I intend that payments of gross income made by the independent Trustees to qualified charitable beneficiaries qualify as income tax charitable deductions. Accordingly, I direct that all provisions of this Paragraph A and this my Will shall be construed to effectuate this intention, that all provisions of this Paragraph A and this my Will shall be construed, and the Foundation be administered, solely in a manner consistent with sections 170(c), 642(c), and 2055 of the Code, and

15

with regulations and rulings which may be promulgated from time to time with respect to trusts creating charitable interests, that none of the powers granted to the Trustees by this my Will shall be exercised in a manner as to disqualify the Foundation for such deductions, and specifically, but without limiting the foregoing, that nothing in this my Will shall be construed to restrict the Trustees from investing the assets of the Foundation in a manner which could result in the annual realization of a reasonable amount of income or gain from the sale or disposition of the assets of the Foundation. I hereby grant to my Executors and the Trustees all the administrative powers necessary to act in compliance with the requirements of the Code, as in effect at the time of my death and from time to time thereafter, so as to qualify the interest committed to the qualified charitable beneficiaries hereunder for the estate and income tax charitable deductions. Should any provisions of this my Will be inconsistent or in conflict with the sections of the Code and the regulations and rulings governing charitable lead trusts as in effect from time to time, then such sections, regulations and rulings shall be deemed to override and supersede such inconsistent or conflicting provisions. If such sections, regulations and rulings at any time require that instruments creating charitable lead trusts contain provisions which are not expressly set forth in this my Will, then such provisions shall be incorporated herein by reference and shall be deemed to be a part of this my Will to the same extent as though they had been expressly set forth herein.

8. <u>Trustees' Limited Power of Amendment</u>. The Trustees shall have the power, acting alone, to amend the provisions governing this Foundation contained in this my Will in any manner required for the sole purpose of ensuring that the Foundation qualifies and continues to qualify as a charitable lead annuity trust.

B. Upon the expiration of the Foundation's primary term the assets of the Foundation (other than any amount due to the qualified charitable beneficiaries) shall be disposed of in the following manner:

1. If no descendant of any child of mine is then living, the assets of the Foundation shall be transferred, conveyed and paid over as follows: (a) one-half (1/2) thereof (or the entire amount thereof if neither my sister, Lee B. Radziwill, nor any descendant of hers is then living) to the then living descendants of my cousin Michel Bouvier, per stirpes; and (b) the other one-half (1/2) thereof (or the entire amount thereof if no descendant of my cousin Michel Bouvier is then living) to the then living descendants of my sister, Lee B. Radziwill, per stirpes, or, if no such descendant of hers is then living, to my said sister, if she shall then be living.

2. If one or more descendants of any child of mine is then living but no such descendant was in being at the time of my death, the assets of the Foundation shall be transferred, conveyed and paid over as follows: (a) one-half (1/2) thereof (or the entire amount if no descendant of my son, John F. Kennedy, Jr., is then living) to the then living descendants of my daughter, Caroline B. Kennedy, per stirpes; and (b) one-half (1/2) thereof (or the entire amount if no descendant of my daughter, Caroline B. Kennedy, is then living) to the then living descendants of my son, John F. Kennedy, Jr., per stirpes.

3. If any descendant of any child of mine is then living and if at least one of those then living descendants was in being at the time of my death, the assets of the Foundation shall be divided into a sufficient number of equal shares so that there shall be set aside one (1) such share for the collective descendants who are then living of my daughter, Caroline B. Kennedy, if any such

descendant is then living, and one (1) such share for the collective descendants who are then living of my son, John F. Kennedy, Jr., if any such descendant is then living, such shares to be disposed of as follows: Each such share shall be transferred, conveyed and paid over to the Trustees hereinafter named to be held in separate trust for a secondary trust term for the benefit of the descendants living from time to time of the child of mine for whose benefit the share has been set aside (such descendants shall hereinafter be referred to as the "beneficiaries"). The secondary term for any particular trust created hereunder shall terminate upon the death of the last to die of the beneficiaries, except that the secondary terms of all trusts created pursuant to this subparagraph 3 shall in all events terminate simultaneously no later than twenty-one (21) years after the death of the last to die of the descendants of my former father-in-law Joseph P. Kennedy who were in being at the time of my death. The Trustees shall manage, invest and reinvest the principal of each trust created hereunder, shall collect the income thereof and shall pay over or apply the net income, to such extent and at such time or times as the independent Trustees (i.e., the Trustees of each particular trust created hereunder other than any Trustee who is also a beneficiary of that trust or of any other trust hereunder and other than any Trustee who has disclaimed any property of my Estate which becomes a part of this trust), in the exercise of sole and absolute discretion, deem advisable, to or for the use of such one or more of the beneficiaries, as the independent Trustees, in the exercise of sole and absolute discretion, determine. Any net income not so paid over or applied shall be accumulated and added to the principal of the trust at least annually and thereafter shall be held, administered and disposed of as a part thereof. I authorize and empower the independent Trustees of each trust created hereunder at any time and from time to time to pay over to any one or more of the beneficiaries, or to apply for his, her or their benefit, out of the principal of such trust, such amount or amounts, including the whole thereof, as the independent Trustees, in the exercise of sole and absolute discretion, deem advisable. Each trust established under this subparagraph 3 shall terminate upon the death of the last to die of the beneficiaries thereof, and, notwithstanding the foregoing, each trust established under this subparagraph 3 shall terminate no later than twenty-one (21) years after the death of the last to die of the descendants of my former father-in-law Joseph P. Kennedy who were in being at the time of my death.

The principal of any trust created hereunder which has terminated by reason of the death of the last to die of the beneficiaries thereof, as such principal is then constituted, shall be transferred, conveyed and paid over to the Trustees of the other trust or trusts created hereunder, if any such trust is still in existence, to be held, administered and disposed of as a part thereof. If no other trust created hereunder is then in existence upon the occurrence of such termination, the principal of the last trust created hereunder to terminate, as then constituted, shall be transferred, conveyed and paid over as follows:

(a) If any descendant of any child of mine is then living, (i) one-half (1/2) thereof (or the entire amount if no descendant of my son, John F. Kennedy, Jr., is then living) to the then living descendants of my daughter, Caroline B. Kennedy, per stirpes; and (ii) one-half (1/2) thereof (or the entire amount if no descendant of my daughter, Caroline B. Kennedy, is then living) to the then living descendants of my son, John F. Kennedy, Jr., per stirpes.

(b) If no descendant of any child of mine is then living, (i) one-half (1/2) thereof (or the entire amount thereof if neither my sister, Lee B. Radziwill, nor any descendant of hers is then living) to the then living descendants of my cousin Michel Bouvier,

19

per stirpes; and (ii) the other one-half (1/2) thereof (or the entire amount thereof if no descendant of my cousin Michel Bouvier is then living) to the then living descendants of my sister, Lee B. Radziwill, per stirpes, or, if no such descendant of hers is then living, to my said sister, if she shall then be living.

Should any trust created hereunder terminate by reason of expiration of a period of twenty-one (21) years after the death of the last to die of the descendants of my former father-in-law Joseph P. Kennedy in being at the time of my death, the principal of each such terminating trust, as then constituted, shall be transferred, conveyed and paid over to the then living beneficiaries of that trust in equal shares.

SIXTH: A. Unless it shall not be permissible under the applicable rules of law to create a trust of the property described in this Paragraph A, if any individual under the age of twenty-one (21) years becomes entitled to any property from my estate upon my death or any property from any trust created hereunder upon the termination thereof, such property shall be held by, and I give, devise and bequeath the same to, the Trustees hereinafter named, IN TRUST, NEVERTHELESS, for the following uses and purposes: To manage, invest and reinvest the same, to collect the income and to apply the net income and principal to such extent (including the whole thereof) for such individual's general use and at such time or times as the Independent Trustees (i.e., the Trustees of each particular trust created hereunder other than any Trustee who is also a beneficiary of that trust or of any other trust hereunder and other than any Trustee who has disclaimed any property of my Estate which becomes a part of this trust), in the exercise of sole and absolute discretion, shall determine, until such individual reaches the age of twenty-one (21) years, and thereupon to transfer, convey and pay over the principal of the trust, as it is then constituted, to such individual. Any net income not so applied shall be accumulated and added to the principal of the trust at least annually and thereafter shall be held, administered and disposed of as a part thereof. Upon the death of such individual before reaching the age of twenty-one (21) years, the Trustees shall transfer, convey and pay over the principal of the trust, as it is then constituted, to such individual's executors or administrators.

If my Executors or the independent Trustees, as the case may be, in the exercise of sole and absolute discretion, determine at any time not to transfer in trust or not to continue to hold in trust any part or all of such property, as the case may be, they shall have full power and authority to transfer and pay over such property, or any part thereof, without bond, to such individual, if an adult under the law of the state of his or her domicile at the time of such payment, or to his or her parent, the guardian of his or her person or property, or to a custodian for such individual under any Uniform Gifts to Minors Act pursuant to which a custodian is acting or may be appointed.

The receipt of such individual, if an adult, or the parent, the guardian or custodian to whom any principal or income is transferred and paid over pursuant to any of the above provisions shall be a full discharge to my Executors or the Trustees, as the case may be, from all liability with respect thereto.

B. If it shall not be permissible under the applicable rules of law to create a trust of the property hereinabove described in Paragraph A, and if such individual is a minor as hereinafter defined, in that event such property shall vest absolutely in such minor, subject to the following: I hereby authorize and empower the Trustees hereinafter named to retain such minor's property without bond, as donees of a power in trust for the following uses and purposes: To manage, invest and reinvest the same, to collect the income and to apply the net income and principal to such extent (including the whole thereof) for such minor's general use and at such time or times as the independent Trustees, in the exercise of sole and absolute discretion, shall determine, until such minor reaches the age of majority, and thereupon to transfer, convey and pay over the property, as it is then constituted, to such minor. Any net income not so applied shall be accumulated and added to principal at least annually and thereafter shall be held, administered and disposed of as a part thereof. Upon the death of such minor before reaching his or her majority, the Trustees shall transfer, convey and pay over the property, as it is then constituted, to such minor's executors or administrators.

If my Executors or the independent Trustees, as the case may be, in the exercise of sole and absolute discretion, determine at any time not to transfer to the Trustees as such donees of a power in trust or not to continue to hold any part or all of such property as hereinabove provided, as the case may be, they shall have full power and authority to transfer and pay over such property or any part thereof, without bond, to such minor's parent or to the guardian of such minor's person or property, or to a custodian for such minor under any Uniform Gift to Minors Act pursuant to which a custodian is acting or may be appointed.

The receipt of the parent, guardian or custodian to whom any property is transferred and paid over pursuant to any of the above provisions shall be a full discharge to my Executors or the Trustees, as the case may be, from all liability with respect thereto.

As compensation for their services under this Paragraph B the Trustees shall be entitled to commissions at the rates and in the manner allowed to trustees of testamentary trusts under the laws of the State of New York in effect from time to time.

In administering any property pursuant to this Paragraph B, the Trustees shall have all of the powers conferred upon them under this Will.

The term "minor" as used in this Paragraph B shall be deemed to refer to an individual under the age at which such individual may execute a binding contract to dispose of real or personal property under the laws of the State of his or her domicile.

SEVENTH: Any application of the net income or principal of any trust herein created may be by the payment of bills rendered for the support, maintenance, education or general welfare of the beneficiary for whose use the application is to be made or by the payment of net income or principal to such person or persons, including, in the case of a minor, his or her parent, the guardian of his or her person or property or the person with whom such minor resides, as the Trustees, in the exercise of sole and absolute discretion, deem appropriate. Any such payment or application may be made without bond, without intervention of any guardian or committee, without order of court, without regard to the duty of any person to support the beneficiary and without regard to any other funds which may be available for the purpose. The receipt of the person or persons to whom any net income or principal is paid pursuant to this Article shall be a full discharge to the Trustees from all liability with respect thereto.

EIGHTH: In the event that any beneficiary or beneficiaries hereunder upon whose survivorship any gift, legacy or devise is conditioned and the person or persons, including myself, upon whose prior death such gift, legacy or devise takes effect shall die simultaneously or under such circumstances as to render it impossible or difficult to determine who survived the other, I hereby declare it to be my will that such beneficiary or beneficiaries shall be deemed not to have survived but to have predeceased such person or persons, and that this my Will and any and all of its provisions shall be construed on such assumption and basis.

NINTH: A. All estate, inheritance, legacy, succession or transfer or other death taxes (including any interest and penalties thereon) imposed by any domestic or foreign taxing authority with respect to all property owned by me at the time of my death and passing under this my Will (other than any generation-skipping transfer tax imposed by Chapter 13 of the Code, or any successor section or statute of like import, and any comparable tax imposed by any other taxing authority) shall be paid without apportionment out of my residuary estate and without apportionment within my residuary estate and with no right of reimbursement from any recipient of any such property. By directing payment of the aforesaid taxes from my residuary estate only in so far as those taxes are generated by property passing under this my Will, it is my express intention that the property over which I possess a general power of appointment and to which I refer in Article FOURTH of this my Will shall bear its own share of such taxes.

B. Should my Estate, after payment of all of my debts and funeral expenses, the expenses of estate administration and the taxes referred to in this Article NINTH, be insufficient to satisfy in full all of the preresiduary bequests and devises which I make under Articles FIRST through THIRD hereof, I direct that the bequests and devises in (1) Paragraphs A, B and C of Article FIRST, (2) Article SECOND and (3) Paragraph A of Article THIRD shall abate last after the abatement of the bequests and devises in Paragraphs D and E of Article FIRST and Paragraphs B, C and D of Article THIRD.

TENTH: A.   My Executors may make such elections under the tax laws (including, but without limitation, any election under Chapter 13 of the Code) as my Executors, in the exercise of sole and absolute discretion, deem advisable, regardless of the effect thereof on any of the interests under this Will, and I direct that there shall be no adjustment of such interests by reason of any action taken by my Executors pursuant hereto.

B.   My Executors may, in the exercise of sole and absolute discretion, disclaim or renounce any interest which I or my estate may have under any other will, under any trust agreement or otherwise.

C.   The determination of my Executors with respect to all elections, disclaimers and renunciations referred to in this Article shall be final and conclusive upon all persons.

D.   I authorize my Executors, in the exercise of sole and absolute discretion, to divide (whether before or after any trust is funded and whether before or after any allocation of GST exemption under section 2631 of the Code is made) any trust or any property used or to be used to fund or augment any trust created under this Will into two or more fractional shares. The shares shall be held and administered by the Trustees as separate trusts, but may be managed and invested in solido. Some of the purposes for granting this authority are to provide an inclusion ratio (within the meaning of section 2642(a) of the Code) of zero for the separate trust receiving the fractional share to which the allocation of GST exemption is made.

Whenever two trusts created under this Will are directed to be combined into a single trust (for example, because property of one trust is to be added to the other trust), whether or not the trusts have different inclusion ratios with respect to any common transferor or have different transferors for generation-skipping transfer tax purposes, the Trustees are authorized, in the exercise of sole and absolute discretion, instead of combining said trusts, to administer them as two separate trusts with identical terms in accordance with the provisions that would have governed the combined trusts. However, the Trustees may manage and invest such separate trusts _in solido_.

The Trustees are authorized, in the exercise of sole and absolute discretion, to combine any one or more trusts with identical terms for an identical beneficiary or beneficiaries created under this Will as a single trust. The Trustees are also authorized, in the exercise of sole and absolute discretion, later to divide such trust as provided above in this Paragraph. Without in any way limiting the sole and absolute discretion of the Trustees granted by this Paragraph, I envision that the Trustees will not elect to combine two or more trusts with different inclusion ratios for generation-skipping transfer tax purposes.

ELEVENTH: In addition to, and not by way of limitation of, the powers conferred by law upon fiduciaries, subject, however, to the directions and prohibitions in Article FIFTH hereof, I hereby expressly grant to my Executors with respect to my estate and the Trustees with respect to each of the trust estates herein created, including any accumulated income thereof, the powers hereinafter enumerated, all of such powers so conferred or granted to be exercised by them as they may deem advisable in the exercise of sole and absolute discretion:

(1) To purchase or otherwise acquire, and to retain, whether originally a part of my estate or subsequently acquired, any and all stocks, bonds, notes or other securities, or any variety of real or personal property, including securities of any corporate fiduciary, or any successor or affiliated corporation, interests in common trust funds and securities of or other interests in investment companies and investment trusts, whether or not such investments be of the character permissible for investments by fiduciaries; and to make or retain any such investment without regard to degree of diversification.

26

(2) To sell (including to any descendant of mine), lease, pledge, mortgage, transfer, exchange, convert or otherwise dispose of, or grant options with respect to, any and all property at any time forming a part of my estate or any trust estate, in any manner, at any time or times, for any purpose, for any price and upon any terms, credits and conditions; and to enter into leases which extend beyond the period fixed by statute for leases made by fiduciaries and beyond the duration of any trust.

(3) To borrow money from any lender, including any corporate fiduciary, for any purpose connected with the protection, preservation or improvement of my estate or any trust estate, and as security to mortgage or pledge upon any terms and conditions any real or personal property of which I may die seized or possessed or forming a part of any trust estate.

(4) To vote in person or by general or limited proxy with respect to any shares of stock or other security; directly or through a committee or other agent, to oppose or consent to the reorganization, consolidation, merger, dissolution or liquidation of any corporation, or to the sale, lease, pledge or mortgage of any property by or to any such corporation; and to make any payments and take any steps proper to obtain the benefits of any such transaction.

(5) To the extent permitted by law, to register any security in the name of a nominee with or without the addition of words indicating that such security is held in a fiduciary capacity; and to hold any security in bearer form.

(6) To complete, extend, modify or renew any loans, notes, bonds, mortgages, contracts or any other obligations which I may owe or to which I may be a party or which may be liens or charges against any of my property, or against my estate, although I may not be liable thereon; to pay, compromise, compound, adjust, submit to arbitration, sell or release any claims or demands of my estate or any trust against others or of others against my estate or any trust upon any terms and conditions, including the acceptance of deeds to real property in satisfaction of bonds and mortgages; and to make any payments in connection therewith.

(7) To make distributions in kind (including in satisfaction of pecuniary bequests) and to cause any distribution to be composed of cash, property or undivided fractional shares in property different in kind from any other distribution without regard to the income tax basis of the property distributed to any beneficiary or any trust.

(8) Whenever no corporate fiduciary is acting hereunder, to place all or any part of the securities which at any time are held by my estate or any trust estate in the care and custody of any bank or trust company with no obligation while such securities are so deposited to inspect or verify the same and with no responsibility for any loss or misapplication by the bank or trust company; to have all stocks and registered securities placed in the name of such bank or trust company or in the name of its nominee; to appoint such bank or trust company agent and attorney to collect, receive, receipt for and disburse any income, and generally to perform the duties and services incident to a so-called "custodian" account; and to allocate the charges and expenses of such bank or trust company to income or to principal or partially to income and partially to principal.

(9) To appoint, employ and remove, at any time and from time to time, any accountants, attorneys, investment counselors, expert advisers, agents, clerks and employees; and to fix and pay their compensation from income or principal or partially from income and partially from principal. Nothing herein contained, however, shall be construed to permit any person or entity to receive compensation in excess of what is reasonable, as defined for purposes of sections 4941(d)(2)(E) and 4945(d)(5) of the Code and under the laws of the State of New York, if such compensation is a charge, directly or indirectly, against any charitable lead trust created hereunder.

(10) Whenever permitted by law, to employ a broker-dealer as custodian for all or any part of the securities at any time held by my estate or any trust estate and to register such securities in the name of such broker-dealer.

(11) With respect to securities in any closely-held corporations, or any interests of my estate or any trust estate in any unincorporated business enterprises, to retain any such securities or interests and to allow any assets of my estate or any trust estate invested in any such corporations or businesses to remain so invested for such time as may appear desirable without liability for any such retention of any such stock, to advance money to any such corporations or businesses in order to aid them in their operations or with the view to maintaining or increasing the value of the interest therein of my estate or any trust estate; to provide for the management, operation and conduct of such businesses, either singly or in conjunction with others interested therein; to engage and delegate duties and powers to any employees, managers or other persons, without liability for any delegation except for negligence in selection; to borrow money for such corporations or businesses, and to secure such loans by a pledge or mortgage not only of interests held in such corporations or businesses but also of any other assets held in my estate or any trust estate; to vote any stock so as to effect the election as an officer or director, or both, of any such corporations of any fiduciary hereunder and also to provide for reasonable compensation to such officer or director (which compensation shall be in addition to and not in lieu of any compensation to which such fiduciary may be entitled for acting hereunder); to enter into agreements for voting trusts and to deposit securities with the voting trustees, to delegate duties to such trustees with all powers of an absolute owner of such stock, to authorize such trustees to incur and pay expenses and receive compensation, and to accept and retain any property received under such agreements; to take business risks in the management, operation, conduct and disposition of any such corporations and business enterprises, notwithstanding that my estate or any trust estate shall have an interest therein; to sell the securities or assets of any such corporations or businesses, or to liquidate, dissolve or otherwise dispose of the same; and to organize, either singly or in conjunction with others, a corporation or corporations to carry on any business enterprise, transferring assets or cash thereto for stock.

(12) To manage, insure against loss, subdivide, partition, develop, improve, mortgage, lease or otherwise deal with any real property or interests therein which may form at any time a part of my estate or any trust estate; to satisfy and discharge or extend the term of any mortgage thereon; to demolish, rebuild, improve, repair and make alterations from time to time in any structures upon any

28

such real property; to plat into lots and prepare any such real property for building purposes; to construct and equip buildings and other structures upon any such real property and to make any and all other improvements of any kind or character whatsoever in connection with the development and improvement thereof; to execute the necessary instruments and covenants to effectuate the foregoing powers, including the granting of options in connection therewith.

(13) To divide any trust created under this Will into one or more separate trusts for the benefit of one or more of the beneficiaries of the trust (to the exclusion of the other beneficiaries) so divided, as the Trustees, in the exercise of sole and absolute discretion, determine and to allocate to such divided trust some or all of the assets of the trust estate for any reason including, but not limited to, enabling any such trust or trusts to qualify as an eligible shareholder of a subchapter S corporation as described in sections 1361(c)(2)(A)(i) or 1361(d)(3) of the Code, as the case may be, or for any other purpose.

(14) To delegate any duties or powers, discretionary or otherwise, to a co-fiduciary for such periods and upon such terms and conditions as may be designated in a written instrument acknowledged in such form as would entitle a deed of real property to be recorded and delivered to such co-fiduciary; and the fiduciary so delegating any duties or powers hereunder shall have no further responsibility with respect to the exercise of such duties or powers so long as such delegation shall remain in effect; and any such delegation shall be revocable by a similar instrument so delivered at any time, provided, however, that no duties or powers described in Paragraph J of Article TWELFTH hereof may be delegated to a Trustee who is a beneficiary of any trust created hereunder.

(15) To manage any trust created hereunder in solido with any other trust created hereunder which has similar terms, conditions and beneficiaries.

(16) To execute and deliver any and all instruments to carry out any of the foregoing powers, no party to any such instrument being required to inquire into its validity or to see to the application of any money or other property paid or delivered pursuant to the terms of any such instrument.

TWELFTH: A. I appoint ALEXANDER D. FORGER and MAURICE TEMPELSMAN Executors of this my Last Will and Testament. If either of them should fail to qualify or cease to act as Executor hereunder, I authorize, but do not direct, the other, in the exercise of sole and absolute discretion, to appoint as a co-Executor such individual or such bank or trust company as he, in the exercise of sole and absolute discretion, shall select. Any such appointment shall be made by an instrument in writing filed with the clerk of the appropriate court.

If at any time and for any reason there is only one Executor acting hereunder, I authorize, but do not direct, such Executor to appoint such individual or such bank or trust company as such Executor, in the exercise of sole and absolute discretion, shall select as successor Executor to act in his or her place if he or she should cease to act. Any such appointment shall be made by an instrument in writing filed with the clerk of the appropriate court and may be revoked by such Executor during his or her lifetime and succeeded by a later appointment, the last such appointment to control.

B. Should it be necessary for a representative of my estate to qualify in any jurisdiction wherein any Executor named herein cannot or may not desire to qualify as such, any other Executor acting hereunder shall, without giving any security, act as Executor in such jurisdiction and shall have therein all the rights, powers, privileges, discretions and duties conferred or imposed upon my Executor by the provisions of this my Will, or, if no Executor can or wishes to qualify as Executor in such other jurisdiction, or, if at any time and for any reason there shall be no Executor in office in such other jurisdiction, I appoint as Executor therein such person or corporation as may be designated by the Executors acting hereunder. Such substituted Executor shall, without giving any security, have in such other jurisdiction all the rights, powers, privileges, discretions and duties conferred or imposed upon my Executors by the provisions of this my Will.

C. I appoint ALEXANDER D. FORGER and MAURICE TEMPELSMAN Trustees of the trust created under Paragraph A of Article SECOND of this my Will. If either of them should fail to qualify or cease to act as a Trustee hereunder, I authorize, but do not direct, the other, in the exercise of sole and absolute discretion, to appoint as a co-Trustee such individual or such bank or trust company as he, in

30

the exercise of sole and absolute discretion, shall select. Any such appointment shall be made by an instrument in writing filed with the clerk of the appropriate court.

If at any time and for any reason there is only one Trustee acting for said trust, I authorize, but do not direct, such Trustee to appoint such individual or such bank or trust company as such Trustee, in the exercise of sole and absolute discretion, shall select as successor Trustee to act in his or her place if he or she should cease to act. Any such appointment shall be made by an instrument in writing filed with the clerk of the appropriate court and may be revoked by such Trustee during his or her lifetime and succeeded by a later appointment, the last such appointment to control.

D. I appoint my daughter, CAROLINE B. KENNEDY, my son, JOHN F. KENNEDY, JR., ALEXANDER D. FORGER and MAURICE TEMPELSMAN Trustees of the trust created under Paragraph A of Article FIFTH of this my Will and therein designated THE C & J FOUNDATION provided, however, that, if my daughter and/or my son disclaims any property of my Estate which becomes part of the trust created under Paragraph A of Article FIFTH, my daughter and/or my son who has so disclaimed shall only serve as an Administrative Trustee. An Administrative Trustee is only authorized to take such actions as are necessary to preserve and maintain the trust property within the meaning of Treas. Reg. § 25.2518-2(d)(2) and, accordingly, is prohibited from participating in the exercise, or decision not to exercise, any discretion over payments, distributions, applications or accumulations of income or principal by the Trustees, including the selection of the charitable beneficiaries of the annuity interest.

Should any one or more of the Trustees herein designated fail to qualify or cease to act as a Trustee of said Foundation without having designated his or her successor in the manner authorized by Paragraph H of this Article, I direct the Trustees or Trustee continuing in office to exercise that right so that there shall be a minimum of two (2) Trustees in office for the Foundation at all times.

E.   I appoint CAROLINE B. KENNEDY and JOHN F. KENNEDY, JR., or the survivor of them, Trustees of each trust created under subparagraph B(3) of Article FIFTH of this my Will provided, however, that, if my daughter and/or my son disclaims any property of my Estate which becomes part of the trust created under Paragraph B(3) of Article FIFTH, my daughter and/or my son who has so disclaimed shall only serve as an Administrative Trustee. An Administrative Trustee is only authorized to take such actions as are necessary to preserve and maintain the trust property within the meaning of Treas. Reg. § 25.2518-2(d)(2) and, accordingly, is prohibited from participating in the exercise, or decision not to exercise, any discretion over payments, distributions, applications or accumulations of income or principal by the Trustees. In addition, I appoint as co-Trustee or co-Trustees of each such trust such person or persons and/or bank or trust company as my son and daughter, or the survivor of them, shall agree upon and designate as co-Trustee or co-Trustees by an instrument in writing to be filed with the clerk of the appropriate court. It shall not be necessary to appoint successors to any individual acting as a Trustee of any trust created under subparagraph B(3) of Article FIFTH hereof if and during such time as a bank or trust company shall be acting hereunder.

F.   I appoint my daughter, CAROLINE B. KENNEDY, and my son, JOHN F. KENNEDY, JR., Trustees of any trust created under Article SIXTH of this my Will, and I authorize any one parent of any individual for whom any such trust is created to qualify as a co-Trustee of such trust if he or she cares to do so provided, however, that, if my daughter and/or my son disclaims any property of my

32

Estate which becomes part of the trust created under Article SIXTH, my daughter and/or my son who has so disclaimed shall only serve as an Administrative Trustee. An Administrative Trustee is only authorized to take such actions as are necessary to preserve and maintain the trust property within the meaning of Treas. Reg. § 25.2518-2(d)(2) and, accordingly, is prohibited from participating in the exercise, or decision not to exercise, any discretion over payments, distributions, applications or accumulations of income or principal by the Trustees.

G. Any Executor or Trustee may resign from office without leave of court at any time and for any reason by filing a written instrument of resignation with the clerk of the appropriate court.

H. I authorize and empower any individual acting as a Trustee of any one or more of the trusts created hereunder to appoint at any time and from time to time any individual or bank or trust company (unless a bank or trust company is then acting as Trustee of such trust) to act as successor Trustee of any one or more of such trusts in the event that the person so making the appointment shall cease to act as a Trustee of such trust or trusts due to his or her death or resignation. If more than one Trustee is acting hereunder, and at any time or from time to time there shall be a vacancy in the office of co-Trustee of any one or more of the trusts created hereunder due to the death or resignation of a co-Trustee and no successor Trustee willing and able to serve shall have been appointed herein or by such co-Trustee as hereinabove provided, then I authorize and empower the remaining individual Trustee, if any, of such trust or trusts to appoint any individual or corporation to act as co-Trustee of such trust or trusts.

I. In the event that the only acting Trustee or Trustees of any trust created hereunder are prohibited from taking certain actions which are necessary or appropriate, I appoint as co-Trustee

33

such individual or bank or trust company as shall be selected, in the exercise of sole and absolute discretion, by the then acting Trustee or Trustees. Any such appointment shall be made by an instrument in writing filed with the clerk of the appropriate court.

J.   Notwithstanding any other provision of this my Will, no Trustee who is a beneficiary of any trust created hereunder or who is under a duty to support a beneficiary shall ever participate in (i) the exercise, or decision not to exercise, any discretion over payments, distributions, applications, accumulations, or uses of income or principal by the Trustees, (ii) the exercise of discretion to allocate receipts or expenses between principal and income, or (iii) the exercise of any general power of appointment described in sections 2041 or 2514 of the Code.

K.   Except as provided by law, I direct that my Executors shall not be required to file any inventory or render any account of my Estate and that no Executor, Trustee, or donee of a power in trust shall be required to give any bond. If, notwithstanding the foregoing direction, any bond is required by any law, statute or rule of court, no sureties shall be required thereon.

L.   I authorize and empower the Trustees or Trustee of each trust created hereunder to transfer the trust assets to, and to hold and administer them in, any jurisdiction in the United States and to account for the same in any court having jurisdiction over said assets.

M.   I direct that any and all powers and discretion conferred by law and by this my Will upon my Trustees including, but not by way of limitation, the right to appoint successor and co-Trustees, may be exercised by the Trustees from time to time qualified and acting hereunder.

N.   Whenever the terms "Executors" or "Executor" and "Trustees" or "Trustee" are used in this my Will, they shall be

34

deemed to refer to the Executors or Executor or the Trustees or Trustee acting hereunder from time to time.

THIRTEENTH: A. A disposition in this Will to the descendants of a person per stirpes shall be deemed to require a division into a sufficient number of equal shares to make one share for each child of such person living at the time such disposition becomes effective and one share for each then deceased child of such person having one or more descendants then living, regardless of whether any child of such person is then living, with the same principle to be applied in any required further division of a share at a more remote generation.

B. As used in this Will, the terms "child," "children," "descendant" and "descendants" are intended to include adopted persons and the descendants of adopted persons, whether of the blood or by adoption.

FOURTEENTH: In accordance with the provisions of section 315(5) of New York's Surrogate's Court Procedure Act, in any proceeding involving my estate or any trust estate created hereunder it shall not be necessary to serve process upon or to make a party to any such proceeding any person under a disability where another party to the proceeding has the same interest as the person under a disability.

FIFTEENTH: No trust created under this my Will shall be subject to the provisions of section 11-2.1(k) of New York's Estates, Powers and Trusts Law (the "EPTL"), nor shall the Trustees of any such trust be obliged to make any allocation to income in respect of any property held as a part of any trust created hereunder which at

..y time is underproductive within the meaning of section 11-2.1(k)(1) of the EPTL.

IN WITNESS WHEREOF, I, JACQUELINE K. ONASSIS, have to this my Last Will and Testament subscribed my name and set my seal this 22 day of March , in the year One Thousand Nine Hundred and Ninety-Four.

Jacqueline K. Onassis

Subscribed and sealed by the Testatrix in the presence of us and of each of us, and at the same time published, declared and acknowledged by her to us to be her Last Will and Testament, and thereupon we, at the request of the said Testatrix, in her presence and in the presence of each other, have hereunto subscribed our names as witnesses this 22nd day of March 1994.

Georgian J. Slade _____ residing at 417 Park Avenue

New York, N.Y.

Samuel S. Polk _____ residing at Succed Hill Road

Bedford, New York

_____ residing at _____

STATE OF NEW YORK   )
                    : ss.:
COUNTY OF New York)

Each of the undersigned, individually and severally being duly sworn, deposes and says:

The within Will was subscribed in our presence and sight at the end thereof by JACQUELINE K. ONASSIS, the within-named Testatrix, on the 22nd day of March , 1994, at 1040 Fifth Avenue

in the State of New York.

Said Testatrix at the time of making such subscription declared the instrument so subscribed to be her Last Will and Testament.

Each of the undersigned thereupon signed his or her name as a witness at the end of said Will at the request of said Testatrix and in her presence and sight and in the presence and sight of each other.

Said Testatrix was, at the time of so executing said Will, over the age of 18 years and, in the respective opinions of the undersigned, of sound mind, memory and understanding and not under any restraint or in any respect incompetent to make a will.

The Testatrix, in the respective opinions of the undersigned, could read, write and converse in the English language and was suffering from no defect of sight, hearing or speech or from any other physical or mental impairment which would affect her capacity to make a valid will. The Will was executed as a single, original instrument and was not executed in counterparts.

Each of the undersigned was acquainted with said Testatrix at said time and makes this affidavit at her request.

The within Will was shown to the undersigned at the time this affidavit was made, and was examined by each of them as to the signature of said Testatrix and of the undersigned.

The foregoing instrument was executed by the Testatrix and witnessed by each of the undersigned affiants under the supervision of *Georgiana J. Steele* an attorney-at-law.

_____

_____

_____

Severally sworn to before me
this 22nd day of March , 1994.

_____
Notary Public

SURROGATE'S COURT OF THE STATE OF NEW YORK
COUNTY OF NEW YORK

Probate proceeding, Will of
JACQUELINE K. ONASSIS,
Deceased.

AFFIDAVIT PROVING A
CORRECT COPY OF THE
WILL FILED FOR PROBATE

File No...

STATE OF NEW YORK }
COUNTY OF NEW YORK } ss.:

We, GEORGIANA J. SLADE

and   VIVIAN R. ROSENBERG   , being duly and

severally sworn, say, each for himself/herself that he/she has carefully compared the foregoing paper(s) with

the original(s) thereof, dated the 22nd   day of March   , 19 94 ,

about to be filed for probate, and that the same in all respects is a true and correct copy of said instrument(s)

and of the whole thereof.

_____
GEORGIANA J. SLADE

_____
VIVIAN R. ROSENBERG

Sworn to before me this 26th

day of May   , 19 94 .

_____
Notary Public

PAULA A. RYAN
NOTARY PUBLIC, State of New York
No. 31-4915328
Qualified in New York County
Commission Expires Nov. 30, 1995

NOTE: Attach a copy of the Will to this affidavit and have the affidavit of comparison executed by any two persons: If a photo copy of the Will is used, only one person need make the affidavit.

S..... 92 Fri 1:16

1. NAME OF DECEASED (Type or Print) JACQUELINE KENNEDY ONASSIS

(First Name) (Middle Name) (Last Name)

MEDICAL CERTIFICATE OF DEATH (To be filled in by the Physician)

2. PLACE OF DEATH	2. NEW YORK CITY 2a. BOROUGH MAN	2b. Name of hospital or other facility (if not facility, street address) 1040 5TH AVE, NYC	2c. If in hospital or other facility 1 ☐ DOA 3 ☐ Outpatient 2 ☐ Emerg. 4 ☐ Inpatient	2d. If inpatient, date of current admission

| | | | | | | Month | Day | Year |

3a. Date and Hour of Death (Month) MAY	(Day) 19	(Year) 1994	3b. HOUR 10	☐ AM ☒ PM	4. SEX F	5. APPROXIMATE AGE 64

6. I HEREBY CERTIFY THAT: (Check One)

☒ I attended the deceased   ☐ A staff physician at this institution attended the deceased

☐ Dr. _____ attended the deceased

from January 15 19 94 to May 19 19 94 and last saw her alive at 10 P M

on May 19 19 94. I further certify that traumatic injury or poisoning DID NOT play any part in causing death, and that death did not occur in any unusual manner and was due entirely to NATURAL CAUSES. See first instruction on reverse of certificate.

Witness my hand this 19 day of May 19 94 Signature Anne Moore D.O. M.D.

Name of Physician Anne Moore, M.D. (Type or Print) Address 520 E 70 ST, NYC

License No. MD 112094

PERSONAL PARTICULARS (To be filled in by Funeral Director or, in case of City Burial, by Physician)

7. Usual Residence a. State New York	7b. County NY	7c. City, Town, or Location New York	7d. Street & House No. 1040 Fifth Avenue	Zip 10028	Apt. No.	7e. Inside City Limits of 7c ☒ Yes ☐ No

8. Served in U.S. Armed Forces No Yes Specify years 0 ☒ 1 ☐ From ___ To ___	9. Marital Status (Check One) 1 ☐ Never Married 2 ☒ Widowed 3 ☐ Married or separated 4 ☐ Divorced	10. Name of Surviving Spouse (If wife, give maiden name)

11. Date of birth (Month) July (Day) 28 (Year) 1929	12. Age at last birthday 64	If under 1 Year mos. / days	If less than 1 Day hours / mins.	13. Social Security No. 578-46-7607

14a. Usual Occupation (Kind of work done during most of working lifetime. Do not enter retired) Editor	14b. Kind of business or industry

15. Birthplace (City & State or Foreign Country) Southampton NY	16. Education (Specify only highest grade completed) Elementary/Secondary (0-12) / College (1-4 or 5+) 5+	17. Other name(s) by which decedent was known

18. NAME OF FATHER OF DECEDENT John V. Bouvier III	19. MAIDEN NAME OF MOTHER OF DECEDENT Janet Lee

20a. NAME OF INFORMANT John F. Kennedy, Jr.	20b. RELATIONSHIP TO DECEASED Son	20c. ADDRESS 1040 Fifth Ave. (CITY) New York (STATE) NY (ZIP) 10028

21a. NAME OF CEMETERY OR CREMATORY Arlington National Cemetery	21b. LOCATION (City, Town, State and Country) Arlington, Virginia	21c. DATE OF BURIAL OR CREMATION May 23, 1994

22a. FUNERAL ESTABLISHMENT F R A N K E C A M P B E L L	22b. ADDRESS 1076 Madison Ave. New York NY 10028

VR15 (1/94) VITAL RECORDS DEPARTMENT OF HEALTH THE CITY OF NEW YORK

CHRONOLOGY

Chronology

July 28, 1929	*Jacqueline Bouvier born in East Hampton, Long Island.*
December 22, 1929	*Baptized at the Church of St. Ignatius Loyola in New York.*
March 3, 1933	*Jackie's sister, Caroline Lee Bouvier, born.*
September 1937	*Jackie's parents separate.*
July 22, 1940	*Divorce between Jackie's parents finalized.*
June 1942	*Jackie's mother is remarried, to Hugh Dudley Auchincloss, Jr.*
Fall 1943	*Jackie starts boarding school at Miss Porter's School in Farmington, Connecticut.*
1945	*Jackie's half-sister, Janet Jennings Auchincloss, born.*
1947	*Jackie's half-brother, James Lee Auchincloss, born.*
May 1947	*Jackie graduates from Miss Porter's.*
Summer 1947	*Jackie's coming-out party held in Newport.*
Fall 1947	*Jackie enrolls at Vassar.*
Fall 1947	*Jackie named "Debutante of the Year" by Igor Cassini*
Summer 1948	*Jackie makes her first trip to Europe with a friend and her Latin teacher from Holton Arms.*
August 1949	*Travels to Paris for her Junior Year Abroad.*
September 1950	*Transfers to George Washington University and graduates the following spring as a French literature major.*

1953

May 1951	*Jackie first meets John F. Kennedy, at a party in Washington.*
Summer 1951	*Wins Vogue's Prix de Paris writing contest with an essay "People I Wish I Had Known." She chose Sergei Dhiagilev, Charles Baudelaire, and Oscar Wilde.*
Summer 1951	*Tours Europe with her sister, Lee Bouvier Radziwill.*
December 1951	*Jackie becomes engaged to John Husted.*
December 1951	*Jackie takes a job at the Washington Times-Herald, quickly moving into the slot of "Inquiring Camera Girl."*
Winter 1951	*Reintroduced to John F. Kennedy, and casual dating begins.*
March 1952	*Jackie calls off engagement with John Husted.*
Summer 1952	*First meeting between Jackie and the Kennedy family.*
January 1953	*Jackie attends Eisenhower's inaugural ball with John F. Kennedy as escort.*
May 1953	*John F. Kennedy proposes to Jackie.*
June 23, 1953	*Engagement announced in newspapers.*
September 12, 1953	*Jackie marries John F. Kennedy at St. Mary's Church in Newport, Rhode Island.*
October 1954	*Kennedy undergoes risky spinal surgery, and Jackie takes up the role of nurse.*
July 1955	*The couple take their first trip to Europe, and Jackie meets Pope Pius XII and the French Premier.*

1963

October 1955	*Jackie's first pregnancy ends in miscarriage.*
January 1956	*Jackie becomes pregnant again.*
August 23, 1956	*Jackie delivers a stillborn daughter by cesarean.*
March 1957	*Jackie becomes pregnant with Caroline.*
Spring 1957	*After living in several different houses, the couple buys a small house on N Street in Georgetown, 3307 N Street, a brick townhouse originally built in 1812.*
August 1957	*Jackie's father dies of liver cancer at the age of 66.*
November 27, 1957	*Jackie gives birth to Caroline Bouvier Kennedy, who is premature but healthy.*
Summer 1958	*John. F. Kennedy runs for the Senate, and Jackie helps with campaigning.*
November 1960	*John F. Kennedy is elected President.*
November 25, 1960	*Jackie gives birth to John F. Kennedy. Jr.*
Fall 1960	*Jackie first named to Eleanor Lambert's International "Best Dressed" list. She would reappear in 1961, 1962, and 1964.*
January 20, 1961	*The new first family moves into the White House.*
May 1961	*First state visit to Europe, with stops in France, London, and Austria.*
Spring 1962	*Jackie gives a live televised tour of the White House to CBS. It is watched by over 46 million viewers.*

1966

March 1962	*Jackie travels to India and Pakistan.*
Summer 1962	*Jackie travels to Italy for a private session with the Pope.*
April 1962	*Jackie organizes White House party for Nobel Prize winners.*
April 18, 1963	*Jackie gives birth to Patrick Bouvier Kennedy, who is seriously underweight and dies three days later.*
September 1963	*Jackie first meets Aritotle Onassis on his yacht in the Mediterranean.*
November 22, 1963	*John F. Kennedy is assassinated as Jackie rides with him through Dallas.*
November 25, 1963	*John F. Kennedy is buried at Arlington National Cemetery.*
November 29, 1963	*The reference to the Kennedy administration as "Camelot" is first made by Jackie in an interview with* Life.
December 1963	*Jackie moves to 3017 N Street in Georgetown, a mansion across the street from the Harriman residence.*
Fall 1964	*After buying an apartment at 1040 Fifth Avenue, Jackie moves to New York.*
1966	*Jackie begins to reappear in public social events.*
June 1968	*Robert F. Kennedy is killed in Los Angeles.*
October 10, 1968	*Jackie marries Aristotle Socrates Onassis on the Greek island of Skorpios.*
Fall 1973	*Strains in the marriage become apparent. Onassis rewrites his will.*
March 15, 1975	*Aristotle Onassis dies in Paris of pneumonia.*
Fall 1975	*Jackie accepts a job as editor for Viking.*

1989

March 1962	*Jackie travels to India and Pakistan.*
Summer 1962	*Jackie travels to Italy for a private session with the Pope.*
April 1962	*Jackie organizes White House party for Nobel Prize winners.*
April 18, 1963	*Jackie gives birth to Patrick Bouvier Kennedy, who is seriously underweight and dies three days later.*
September 1963	*Jackie first meets Aritotle Onassis on his yacht in the Mediterranean.*
November 22, 1963	*John F. Kennedy is assassinated as Jackie rides with him through Dallas.*
November 25, 1963	*John F. Kennedy is buried at Arlington National Cemetery.*
November 29, 1963	*The reference to the Kennedy administration as "Camelot" is first made by Jackie in an interview with* Life.
December 1963	*Jackie moves to 3017 N Street in Georgetown, a mansion across the street from the Harriman residence.*
Fall 1964	*After buying an apartment at 1040 Fifth Avenue, Jackie moves to New York.*
1966	*Jackie begins to reappear in public social events.*
June 1968	*Robert F. Kennedy is killed in Los Angeles.*
October 10, 1968	*Jackie marries Aristotle Socrates Onassis on the Greek island of Skorpios.*
Fall 1973	*Strains in the marriage become apparent. Onassis rewrites his will.*
March 15, 1975	*Aristotle Onassis dies in Paris of pneumonia.*
Fall 1975	*Jackie accepts a job as editor for Viking.*

1989

Fall 1977	*Christina Onassis settles Jackie's suit over her inheritance. Jackie receives 20 million dollars.*
1977	*Resigns as editor of Viking amid controversies over Jeffrey Archer's* Shall We Tell the President?
Spring 1978	*Jackie takes up an editorial post at Doubleday.*
1978	*Jackie buys 365 acres of land on Martha's Vineyard.*
1988	*Maurice Tempelsman moves into Jackie's Fifth Avenue apartment.*
December 11, 1988	*Jackie's first grandchild, Rose Schlossberg, is christened at St. Thomas More church in Manhattan.*
January 1994	*Jackie is diagnosed with lymphoma.*
May 19, 1994	*Jacqueline Kennedy Onassis dies at her Fifth Avenue apartment.*
May 23, 1994	*Jackie is buried at Arlington Cemetery next to John F. Kennedy, after a private funeral service in Manhattan.*
October 7, 1994	*Final headstone for Jackie laid at Arlington.*
April 23-26, 1996	*Many of Jackie's personal items are auctioned at Sotheby's in New York.*